This
Nature Storybook
belongs to:

WALKER BOOKS

First published 1994 by Walker Books Ltd
87 Vauxhall Walk, London SE11 5HJ

This edition published 2009

10 9 8 7 6 5 4 3 2

Text © 1994 Foxbusters Ltd
Illustrations © 1994 Anita Jeram

The right of Dick King-Smith and Anita Jeram
to be identified as author and illustrator respectively
of this work has been asserted by them in accordance
with the Copyright, Designs and Patents Act 1988

This book has been typeset in Baskerville

Printed in China

British Library Cataloguing in Publication Data:
a catalogue record for this book is available from the British Library

ISBN 978-1-4063-1872-2

www.walker.co.uk

I Love Guinea-pigs

Written by
Dick King-Smith

Illustrated by
Anita Jeram

WALKER BOOKS
AND SUBSIDIARIES
LONDON • BOSTON • SYDNEY • AUCKLAND

There's a silly old saying that
if you hold a guinea-pig up
by its tail, its eyes
will drop out.

Well of course they wouldn't,

even if you could. Which you couldn't,

because guinea-pigs don't have tails.

What do guinea-pigs
have in common with pigs?

The males and females are
known as "boars" and "sows".

And they aren't pigs either.

They're rodents – like mice and rats

and squirrels.

Rodents have special front teeth
which are brilliant for gnawing things.
These teeth go on growing throughout
the animal's life, and are self-sharpening.

As for the other bit of their name, guinea-pigs were first brought to Europe about four hundred years ago by Spanish sailors, probably from a country in South America called Dutch Guiana. And the sailors called them "guiana pigs".

In fact the guinea-pig is a member
of the cavy family, and its
Latin name is *Cavia porcellus*
(which means a piggy-looking cavy).

Anyway, whatever they're called,

it's the way they look that I've

always liked. They're so

chunky and chubby

and cuddly, with their blunt

heads and sturdy bodies and short legs.

Smooth

Peruvian

They come in loads of different colours, and they can be smooth-coated or rough-coated or long-coated, not to mention the other varieties.

Crested

Sheltie

I've kept hundreds of guinea-pigs over the last fifty years, but I've always liked the Abyssinians best.

Abyssinians

Guinea-pigs are such sensible animals.

They're awfully easy to keep,

because they aren't fussy.

They don't like the cold, of course, or the damp, any more  than you would, and they're not happy living in a poky little place, any more than you would be. But as long as they have a comfortable warm dry place to live, guinea-pigs are as happy as Larry.

Guinea-pigs like a really big roomy hutch, or, better still, a wire run out on the grass.

They're hardy animals, and don't often fall ill. Properly looked after, they can live a long time.

Most guinea-pigs live for around five to eight years.

I once had a Crested sow
called Zen. She lived two years
with me and then eight more
with one of my daughters.
People's hair grows whiter
as they age, but Zen's
grew darker.

Guinea-pigs need
plenty of food.

They love eating, just like you do, and feeding
them is half the fun of keeping them.

Some people, of course, feed them
nothing but hay and pellets from
the pet shop and they're quite all
right. But how boring a diet like that must
be, both for the piggy-looking
cavy and its
owner.

I always used to give my
guinea-pigs lots of other kinds
of food as well: cabbage and cauliflower leaves,
carrots, bits of bread and apple peelings, and
wild plants like dandelion
and clover. I gave them
water, too, of course.

Guinea-pigs need
clean drinking
water every day. And their water
bottle often needs washing,
because they like blowing bits
of food back up the spout.

One especially nice thing
about guinea-pigs is that
if you handle them
regularly, and carry them about, stroke
them, talk to them, and make a fuss
of them, they become really
fond of you.

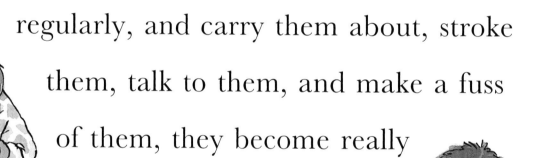

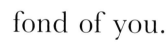

The proper way to pick up a guinea-pig is with one hand over its shoulders and the other supporting its bottom.

19

Another nice thing about
guinea-pigs is that they
talk a lot.

When they want food or water,

they often give a sort of whistle,

sometimes low,

sometimes loud.

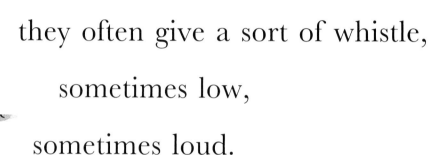

Boars say CHUTTER
when they're squaring
up for a fight.

So do sows when their babies
pester them too much.

Other things guinea-pigs say are

PUTT

CHUT

TWEET

and DRR.

But when one guinea-pig says PURR to another

guinea-pig, it's as plain as the nose on your face

that it only means one thing:

"I love you."

And that brings me on
to what's best of all about
keeping guinea-pigs – baby ones.
Because their ancestors, the wild cavies
of South America, lived out in the
open with enemies all about them,
their young ones had to be
ready to run for it.

So the guinea-pig sow carries
her unborn litter for a very
long time, about seventy days,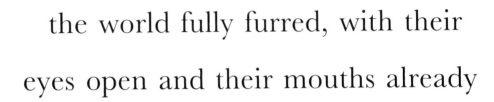
and they arrive in
the world fully furred, with their
eyes open and their mouths already
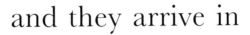
filled with teeth.
Newborn guinea-pigs
are such a comical sight.
Their heads and feet look too big for their bodies.

Baby rabbits are born blind and naked and helpless, but not baby guinea-pigs.

But almost immediately

they show an interest in those two

favourite guinea-pig pursuits –

 eating

and conversation.

Of all the guinea-pigs I've kept,
there were two that I shall never
forget. Both were Abyssinians,
both were boars, and each in his
time fathered dozens of lovely
big-headed, big-footed babies.

One was a bright golden colour, and his name was King Arthur. The other was a blue roan called Beach Boy. Both are buried in my garden.

There's a solitary apple tree at the edge
of my lawn, and I like to look at it and think
that under it Beach Boy and King Arthur
lie peacefully, one on one side of the tree,
one on the other.

I'm not sad about this –
just happy to remember
what a lot of pleasure
I've had from all
my guinea-pigs.

INDEX

Look up the pages to find out
about all these guinea-pig things.
Don't forget to look at both kinds
of words: this kind and **this kind**.

Which of these Nature Storybooks have you read?

Growing Frogs
ISBN 978-1-4063-1206-5

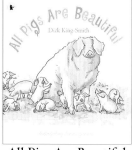
All Pigs Are Beautiful
ISBN 978-1-4063-1196-9

One Tiny Turtle
ISBN 978-1-4063-1198-3

Think of an Eel
ISBN 978-1-4063-1201-0

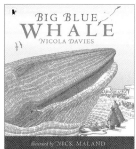
Big Blue Whale
ISBN 978-1-4063-1257-7

Caterpillar Butterfly
ISBN 978-1-4063-1277-5

A Field Full of Horses
ISBN 978-1-4063-1280-5

Bat Loves the Night
ISBN 978-1-4063-1275-1

T. Rex
ISBN 978-1-4063-1290-4

Surprising Sharks
ISBN 978-1-4063-1287-4

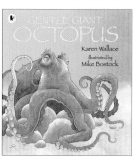
Gentle Giant Octopus
ISBN 978-1-4063-1284-3

Tigress
ISBN 978-1-4063-1296-6

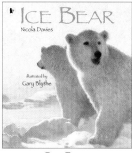
Ice Bear
ISBN 978-1-4063-1304-8

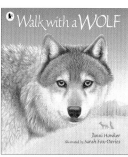
Walk with a Wolf
ISBN 978-1-4063-1308-6

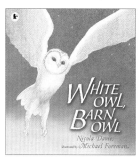
White Owl, Barn Owl
ISBN 978-1-4063-1312-3

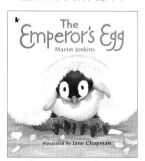
The Emperor's Egg
ISBN 978-1-4063-1301-7

Tracks of a Panda
ISBN 978-1-4063-1871-5

Seahorse: the Shyest Fish in the Sea
ISBN 978-1-4063-2010-7

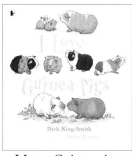
I Love Guinea-pigs
ISBN 978-1-4063-1872-2

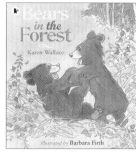
Bears in the Forest
ISBN 978-1-4063-1870-8